MODERN WEAPONS
COMPARED AND CONTRASTED

NAVAL VESSELS

Martin J. Dougherty

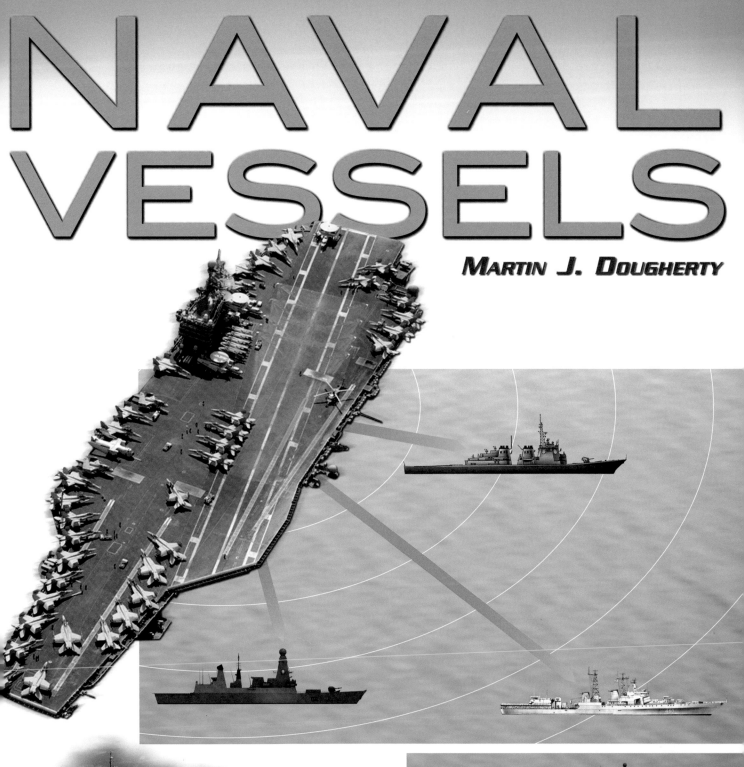

rosen publishing's
rosen central

New York

This edition first published in 2013 by:

The Rosen Publishing Group, Inc.
29 East 21st Street
New York, NY 10010

Additional end matter copyright © 2013 by The Rosen Publishing Group, Inc.

Library of Congress Cataloging-in-Publication Data

Dougherty, Martin J.
Naval vessels/Martin J. Dougherty. —1st ed.
    p. cm.—(Modern weapons: compared and contrasted)
Includes bibliographical references and index.
ISBN 978-1-4488-9248-8 (library binding)
1. Warships. 2. Submarines (Ships) I. Title.
V765.D68 2013
623.825—dc23

                                                                    2012034790

Manufactured in the United States of America

CPSIA Compliance Information: Batch #W13YA: For further information, contact Rosen Publishing, New York, New York, at 1-800-237-9932.

Contents

Introduction

The seas are vitally important to international trade and can be used to project power into distant areas. Controlling a sea area, or at least denying it to the enemy, is a vital part of maritime strategy. Naval forces must deal with threats from submarines, surface vessels and aircraft, necessitating a mixed armament and the sensor systems to make these weapons useful.

A cheap, lightly armed vessel can undertake patrol work and "show the flag" but may be vulnerable to attack. Conversely, an excessively complex or expensive vessel may not justify its cost, especially if the owning nation has extensive commitments. Thus most navies operate a range of vessels, most of which can undertake a variety of duties. Few navies can afford enough specialist ships to ensure that one is available to meet any given situation; for this reason multi-role vessels are currently popular as they provide at least a modest capability in all areas.

LEFT: USS *Seawolf* (SSN-21), lead boat of the US Navy's Seawolf class of nuclear attack submarines, conducts sea trials off the coast of Connecticut. The aerial image shows the sail from a starboard angle, looking forward.

CHAPTER 1

Corvettes and Patrol Craft

Speed and Displacement

▶ **Visby Class**
▶ **Houbei Class**
▶ **Eilat Class**

Large ocean-going warships are inefficient in some applications, such as the defense of a coastline or patrol operations close to the shore. A much smaller and less expensive vessel can provide a credible deterrent in the form of an "armed presence" and can deal with most minor incidents. There is a limit to the amount of weaponry that can be crammed into a small hull of course, but these smaller vessels can still pose a threat to a major warship.

Today's small surface combatants are generally armed with highly effective anti-ship missiles, which can cripple or even sink a major warship. It does not matter how large or small, expensive or basic the launching platform is; what matters is its ability to get its missiles into a suitable firing position. Speed is important when attempting an interception or trying, get into missile range, as an effective set of defenses.

Anti-aircraft and anti-missile defenses in the form of decoys, electronic countermeasures, missiles and guns can all increase the survivability of a surface vessel, but perhaps the best defense of all is not to be attacked. Modern corvettes such as the Visby class and missile boats such as the Chinese Houbei class are designed to have a minimal radar return. Their "stealth" is in part due to small size, and partly due to the use of shaping and advanced materials to absorb or scatter radar energy rather than returning a clear signal.

ABOVE: The Swedish Visby-class corvette is clearly a "stealth boat." It has a minimum of angles and projections to reflect radar energy and uses angled planes to prevent a clean return. It is not invisible to radar but can only be detected at relatively short range, which may enable it to launch a surprise attack.

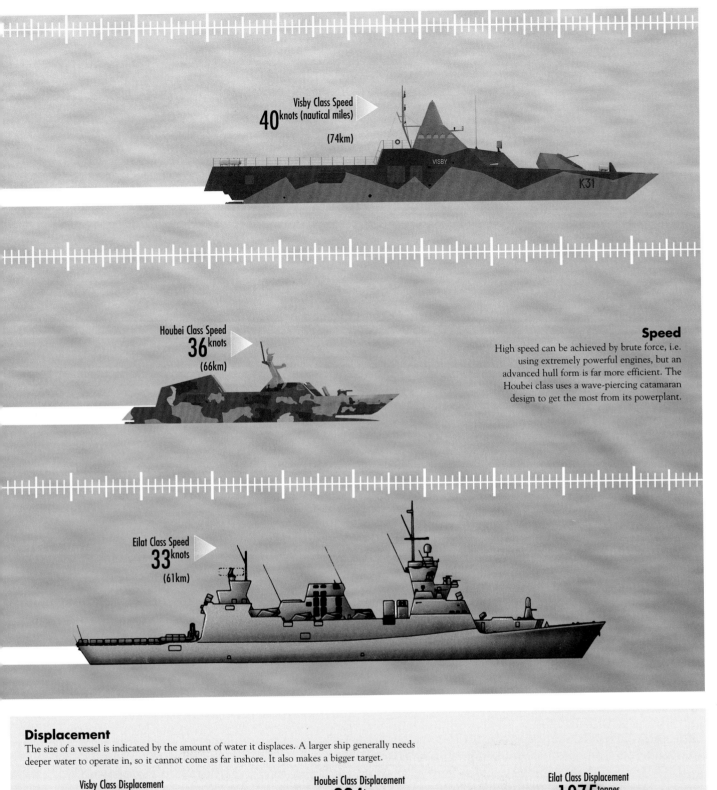

Visby Class Speed
40 knots (nautical miles)
(74km)

VISBY
K31

Houbei Class Speed
36 knots
(66km)

Speed

High speed can be achieved by brute force, i.e. using extremely powerful engines, but an advanced hull form is far more efficient. The Houbei class uses a wave-piercing catamaran design to get the most from its powerplant.

Eilat Class Speed
33 knots
(61km)

Displacement

The size of a vessel is indicated by the amount of water it displaces. A larger ship generally needs deeper water to operate in, so it cannot come as far inshore. It also makes a bigger target.

Visby Class Displacement
640 tonnes
(630 tons)

Houbei Class Displacement
224 tonnes
(220 tons)

Eilat Class Displacement
1075 tonnes
(1058 tons)

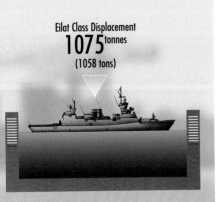

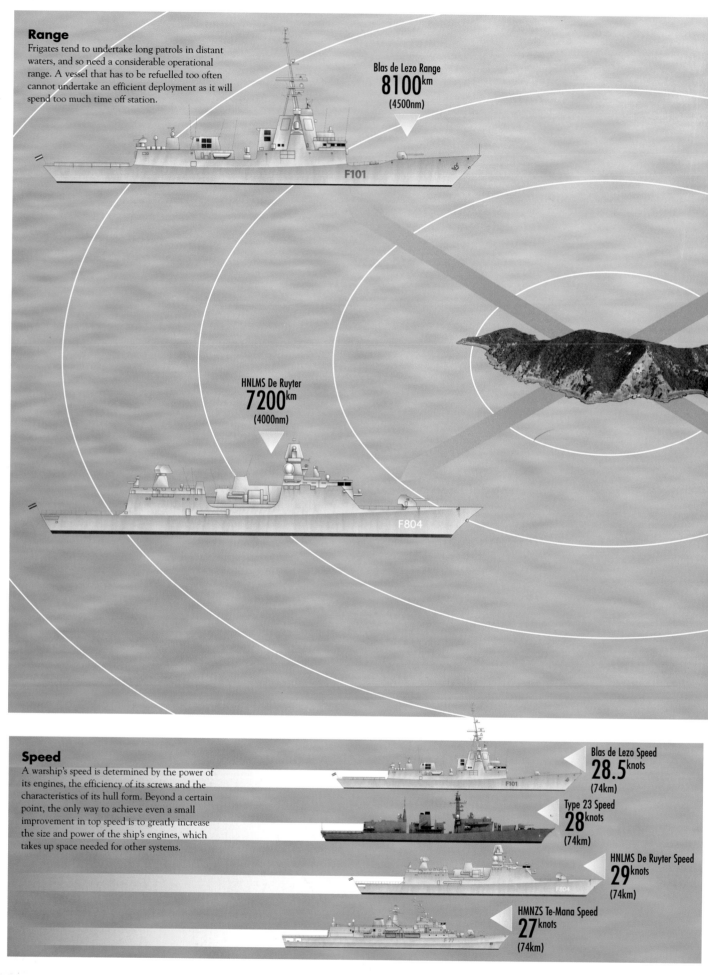

Range

Frigates tend to undertake long patrols in distant waters, and so need a considerable operational range. A vessel that has to be refuelled too often cannot undertake an efficient deployment as it will spend too much time off station.

Blas de Lezo Range
8100km
(4500nm)

HNLMS De Ruyter
7200km
(4000nm)

Speed

A warship's speed is determined by the power of its engines, the efficiency of its screws and the characteristics of its hull form. Beyond a certain point, the only way to achieve even a small improvement in top speed is to greatly increase the size and power of the ship's engines, which takes up space needed for other systems.

Blas de Lezo Speed
28.5knots
(74km)

Type 23 Speed
28knots
(74km)

HNLMS De Ruyter Speed
29knots
(74km)

HMNZS Te-Mana Speed
27knots
(74km)

CHAPTER 2

Frigates 1

Speed and Range

▶ **Blas de Lezo**
▶ **Type 23**
▶ **HNLMS De Ruyter**
▶ **HMNZS Te-Mana**

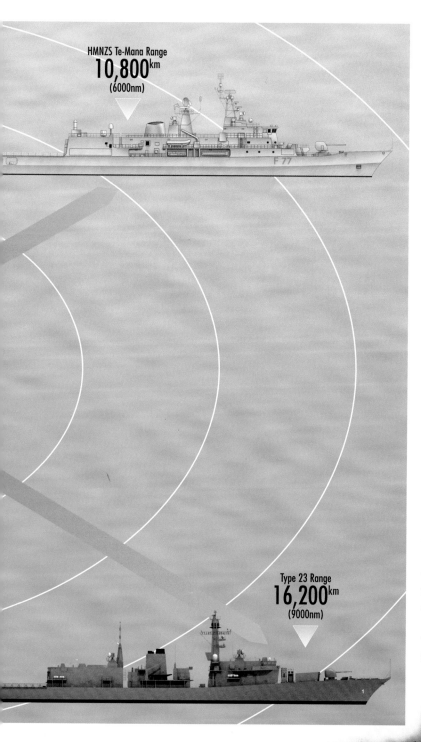

HMNZS Te-Mana Range
10,800km
(6000nm)

F 77

Type 23 Range
16,200km
(9000nm)

Ocean-going warships must cover great distances just to reach their deployment areas, and their maximum range is calculated on the assumption that an economical speed is to be maintained. This range is the maximum distance the vessel can cover in a round trip. It must be sufficient to reach the operational area, carry out the mission and return to port. Fuel is constantly being used up, even when patrolling at a modest speed, and it is rarely useful to anchor in one place for any length of time. Although a range listed in thousands of nautical miles (knots, or nm) may seem like a long way, the oceans are vast and fuel supplies are a constant concern to a ship's captain.

High-speed operations will rapidly deplete fuel reserves and could theoretically leave the vessel stranded. More likely, it would be necessary to reduce speed and break off operations to seek fuel once levels became too low. If replenishment ships are available while underway, a warship's range is enormously increased as it can be refuelled without returning to port, which permits a greater period of high-speed maneuvering.

Despite not being fuel efficient, high speed is vital to a warship, and consequently most vessels in the same general class tend to have a similar top speed. This enables them to pursue and intercept a contact, and to get into (or out of) weapons range as quickly as possible.

RIGHT: The British Type 23 frigate proved to be a versatile type, capable of anti-submarine warfare, warfighting, peacekeeping and maritime security operations across the globe. In recent years, 13 were still in service: three with the Chilean Navy, and 10 with the Royal Navy.

CHAPTER 3

Frigates 2

Complement and Full-load Displacement

▶ **Blas de Lezo**
▶ **Type 23**
▶ **HNLMS De Ruyter**
▶ **HMNZS Te-Mana**

The term "frigate" has meant different things at various times in history. Today, a frigate is a workhorse vessel capable of undertaking a variety of roles. Frigates may operate independently or escort high-value vessels. They must be capable of dealing with submarine, air and surface threats, though many designs are optimized for one of these roles and retain the others as a secondary capability. Thus a frigate must carry a mix of guns, missiles and torpedoes, plus helicopters and the specialist sensors required to track surface, air and underwater targets. All these systems require specialist crew members to operate and maintain them. Recent frigate designs include a number of innovative measures designed to improve efficiency. Thus the British Type 23, which was developed as an anti-submarine platform at the end of the 1970s, requires far more crew members to operate it than the multi-role FREMM frigate recently designed by France and Italy, despite the FREMM class ships being much larger. However, automation is not the only factor that determines a ship's displacement and the crew size needed. Greater capability always comes at the cost of increased displacement and crew requirements.

Complement

Adding a weapon or sensor system requires not only personnel to man it, but also increases the quantity of support personnel and supplies the vessel must carry. Machinery can only go so far towards replacing people, after which the vessel becomes critically vulnerable to casualties or fatigue due to overwork.

Blas de Lezo Complement
250 men

Type 23 Complement
181 men

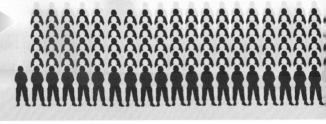

HNLMS De Ruyter Complement
202 men

LEFT: Modern frigates such as the Type 23 are light, fast and maneuverable.

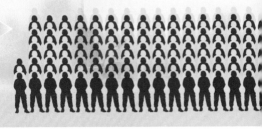

HMNZS Te-Mana Complement
163 men

Full-load Displacement

One way to keep displacement down is to create a vessel with deliberately limited capabilities or one optimized for a single role with only a token capability in other areas. However, this can lead to a vessel simply being too small to accommodate necessary new equipment as operational requirements change.

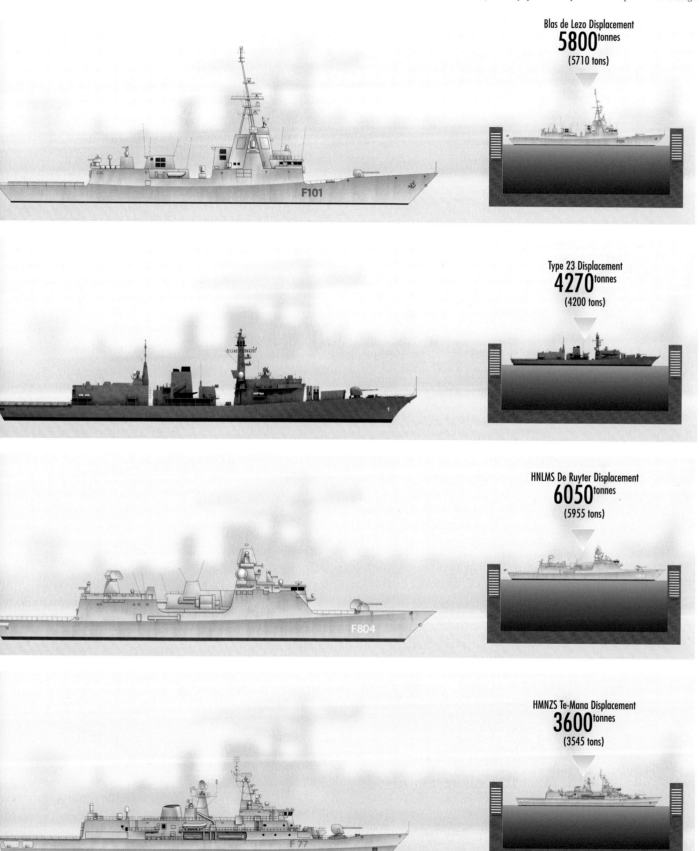

Blas de Lezo Displacement
5800 tonnes
(5710 tons)

Type 23 Displacement
4270 tonnes
(4200 tons)

HNLMS De Ruyter Displacement
6050 tonnes
(5955 tons)

HMNZS Te-Mana Displacement
3600 tonnes
(3545 tons)

Anti-Submarine Torpedoes

Modern anti-submarine torpedoes have to be able to track and hit a deep-diving submarine in open water and also function in the cluttered and confusing shallow-water environment close to shore. Older weapons lacked one or both of these capabilities, limiting their usefulness.

Type 054A
7.3km
(4.5 miles)

CHAPTER 4

Frigates: Anti-Submarine Warfare

Torpedo Range

▶ **Type 23**
▶ **Sachsen Class**
▶ **Type 054A**

Detonation
If a contact detonation is accomplished, the warhead does not need to be especially big to do crippling or fatal damage. Submarines are not armored; their best defense lies in remaining undetected or denying the enemy a clear signature to home in on.

Type 23
11 km
(6.8 miles)

Sachsen Class
10 km
(6.2 miles)

RIGHT: The *Sachsen* receives supplies. The anti-submarine role has traditionally been a job for frigates. Most classes carry at least one helicopter to extend their sensor reach with "dipping" sonar and to deliver an attack against a distant contact. Helicopter-delivered torpedoes are normally the same as those launched from warships.

In the past, a range of anti-submarine weapons have been used, including depth charges dropped over the stern of a surface vessel or fired from a launcher. Rockets and mortars have also been used to scatter contact-fused bombs over the suspected position of a submarine. These measures required the surface vessel to approach very closely, whereas torpedoes greatly increase the reach of the anti-submarine vessel.

Most frigates engage submarines using lightweight torpedoes from deck-mounted launchers. The weapons have a significant range, but this is exceeded by that of a heavyweight guided torpedo from a submarine. However, it is not just the range of the weapons that dictates the distance at which the vessel can engage; it is also the efficiency of its sensors. A stealthy submarine may not be detected until it is fairly close, reducing the effectiveness of long-range anti-submarine weapons.

An anti-submarine torpedo must be fast enough to reach the target before it moves out of range, and must be able to home in on a stealthy boat that is trying to creep away. Its targeting processor must be sophisticated enough to discern the real signature of the boat from background ocean noise, decoys and other distractions.

HMS Edinburgh

Murasame

Brandenburg

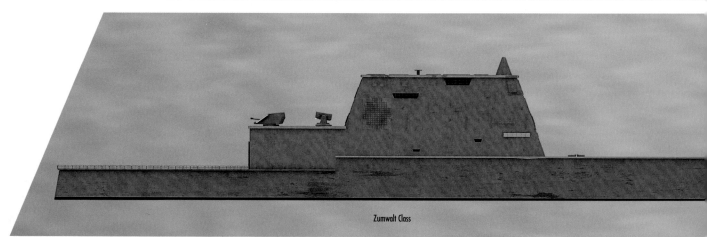

Zumwalt Class

Armament

Besides a recent tendency towards larger guns, there has been a move from fixed or trainable missile launchers to vertical-launch systems (VLS). A VLS system can launch several different types of missiles and can deliver the salvo much faster than a trainable launcher that has to be reloaded. VLS systems have no blind arcs blocked by the ship's superstructure, as the missile climbs above the vessel before turning towards the target.

Sea Dart launcher
1

114mm (4.5in) gun
1

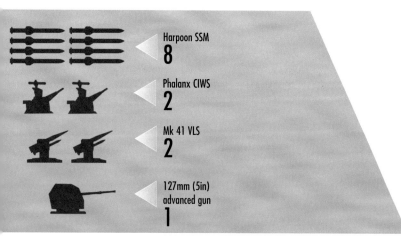

Harpoon SSM
8

Phalanx CIWS
2

Mk 41 VLS
2

127mm (5in) advanced gun
1

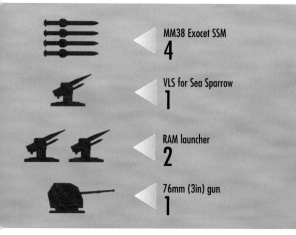

MM38 Exocet SSM
4

VLS for Sea Sparrow
1

RAM launcher
2

76mm (3in) gun
1

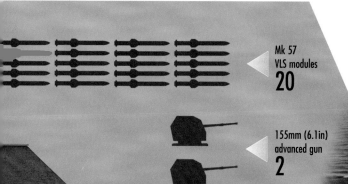

Mk 57 VLS modules
20

155mm (6.1in) advanced gun
2

CHAPTER 5

Guided Missile Destroyers

Armament

▶ **HMS *Edinburgh* (Type 42)**
▶ **Murasame**
▶ **Brandenburg**
▶ **Zumwalt Class**

Destroyers were originally developed to protect the battle line from torpedo boats (hence their original name of "torpedo-boat destroyers"). They soon developed into general-purpose light warships equipped with guns and torpedoes, capable of undertaking offensive and defensive operations. Over time, as the battleship has passed away, destroyers have gone from being fleet escorts to the primary warships fielded by many nations. Today's destroyers are primarily concerned with surface action, air defense and attacks against shore targets, using a mix of guns and missiles.

The guns shipped by modern destroyers are usually similar in caliber to those traditionally carried, but most ships have just one or two rather than mounting several turrets as was common in World War II designs. There has recently been a move towards larger and more powerful guns, largely for shore bombardment. Thus the recent Zumwalt class carries much more powerful guns than the earlier Type 42 class such as *Edinburgh*.

BELOW: The hull form of the US Zumwalt-class destroyer is optimized for stealth. By using vertical-launch missile systems, its designers reduced the number of corners and projections above the decks, which in turn reduced radar return, making the vessel hard to detect.

CHAPTER 6

Destroyers

Speed and Range

▶ **HMS *Daring* (Type 45)**
▶ **Kongo**
▶ **Udaloy Class**

The line between different classes of warship has become increasingly blurred in recent years. Displacement is no longer the defining factor; some vessels designated as frigates are larger than certain destroyer classes. There is also a significant overlap in terms of role – specialist vessels optimized for anti-submarine and anti-aircraft work exist in both the frigate and destroyer classes. The issue is further confused when one navy assigns a designation to a class that has a different name in its parent navy. The Udaloy class was termed a "large anti-submarine ship" by its Russian designers, which exactly described its designed role. Western observers designated it a destroyer, based mainly on its size.

As a general rule, destroyers are larger, more capable and more expensive than frigates, and tend to operate as part of a task force rather than independently. They also tend to have more extensive anti-air and anti-surface armament, though this depends greatly upon the operating navy. Few navies have any larger surface combatants, other than aircraft carriers, so the guided missile destroyer has stepped into the role of a capital ship in many areas.

As a significant naval asset, a destroyer requires a large operational radius and must be capable of high speed in order to pursue or evade hostile vessels. Although missiles do have a long range, the sensors that locate targets for them are often more limited and must be brought within range of an enemy force. High speed enables a destroyer to comply with the most basic of naval strategies – to attack effectively first.

HMS Daring Range
12,600km
(7000nm)

BELOW: Aircraft are one of the primary threats to modern naval forces, and the Kongo class destroyer is designed to protect itself and other vessels from attack. It can track large numbers of airborne targets simultaneously, engaging them with medium-range and short-range missiles as necessary.

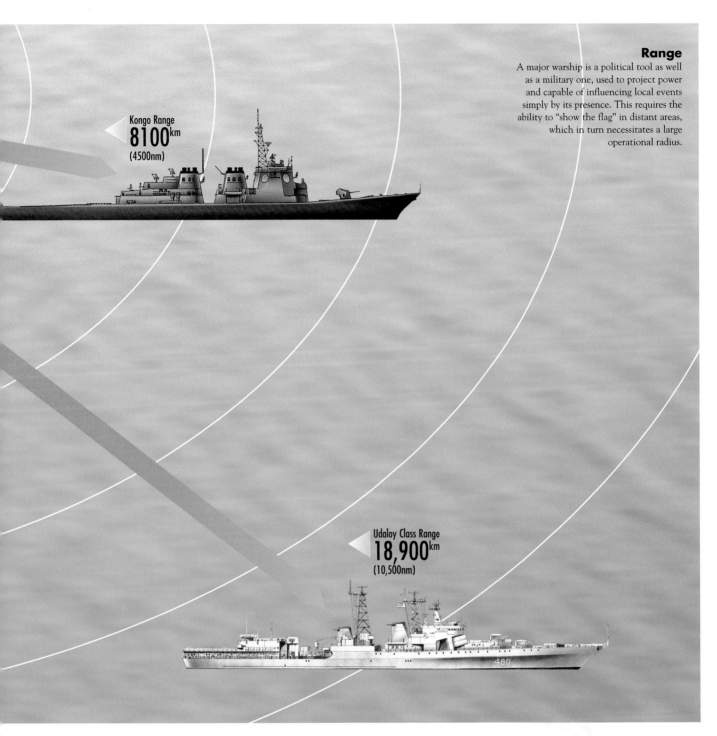

Range

A major warship is a political tool as well as a military one, used to project power and capable of influencing local events simply by its presence. This requires the ability to "show the flag" in distant areas, which in turn necessitates a large operational radius.

Kongo Range
8100km
(4500nm)

Udaloy Class Range
18,900km
(10,500nm)

Speed

It was once considered that "speed is armor," but, in an age of guided missiles, this is no longer the case. However, high speed does enable a warship to rapidly close to optimum firing range for its weapons, hopefully breaking the "kill chain" by disabling enemy vessels before they can attack.

HMS *Daring* Speed
29knots
(52.2km/h)

Kongo Speed
30knots
(54km/h)

Udaloy Class Speed
35knots
(63km/h)

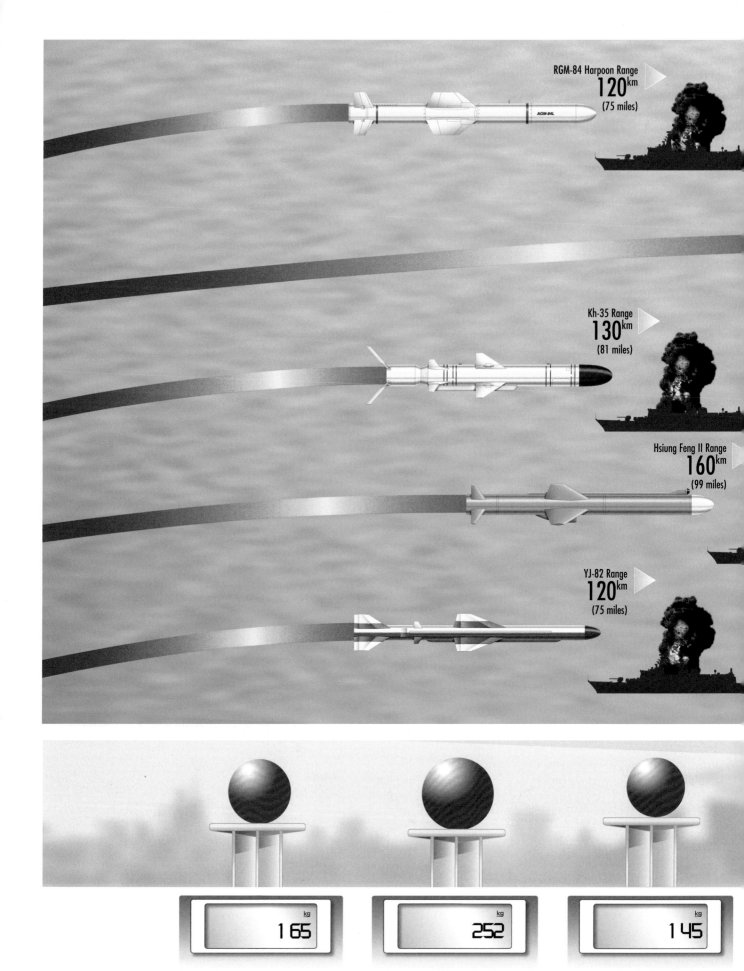

RGM-84 Harpoon Range
120^{km}
(75 miles)

Kh-35 Range
130^{km}
(81 miles)

Hsiung Feng II Range
160^{km}
(99 miles)

YJ-82 Range
120^{km}
(75 miles)

kg
165

kg
252

kg
145

YJ-82 Warhead: 165kg (364lb)

Hsiung Feng II Warhead: 252kg (556lb)

Kh-35 Warhead: 145kg (320lb)

Range

Missile ranges often greatly exceed the range of radar systems carried aboard warships. Targeting information can be obtained from other platforms such as helicopters, reconnaissance aircraft or other ships. Targeting data plus effective missiles is a winning formula; lack of either makes the other useless.

RSB-15F Range
250km
(155 miles)

RSB-15F Warhead: 200kg (441lb)

RGM-84 Harpoon Warhead: 221kg (487lb)

200 kg

221 kg

CHAPTER 7

Ship-to-Ship Missiles

Range and Warhead Weight

▶ **RGM-84 Harpoon**

▶ **RSB-15F**

▶ **Kh-35**

▶ **Hsiung Feng II**

▶ **YJ-82**

Long-range missiles are the primary surface-action weapons carried by warships, with guns and shorter-range missiles available as a back-up. A force that lacks long-range capability may not survive long enough to make an attack; in modern naval combat, victory usually goes to the side that can attack effectively first. This means detecting the enemy force, reaching a suitable firing position and delivering a missile strike before the enemy can launch his own weapons.

Most missiles use either thermal homing or radar guidance for terminal guidance, and are thus vulnerable to electronic countermeasures or decoys. Missiles can also be shot down by anti-aircraft missiles or close-in weapons systems (CIWS), which are designed to deal with small, fast-moving targets. If a hit is achieved, the missile will detonate after penetrating the target, to ensure that maximum damage is caused. Even so, a single hit is not guaranteed to sink a warship. Ships are very resilient even when hit in a vital area, and a missile might detonate in a non-critical part of the vessel.

Warhead size is important for ensuring that enough damage is done, but there is a trade-off between the weight and size of the warhead and the amount of propellant carried by the missile. A larger warhead means a shorter range, giving the advantage to an enemy whose missiles have a longer reach. A larger missile may be an option, but space is limited aboard a warship. Bigger missiles may mean less of them, which reduces the chances of getting through the target's defenses.

Warhead Weight

Although missile waheads do not need to penetrate the thick armor of previous generations of warships, they need to be powerful enough to do serious damage to the target. Warships are designed to withstand shock and are heavily compartmentalized to contain damage. Ideally, a warhead will breach as many compartments as possible, which requires a large amount of explosive.

Full-load Displacement

The United States is the only nation to operate huge "supercarriers" capable of operating a very large air group. Greater displacement equates to a longer flight deck, enabling heavier aircraft to be deployed.

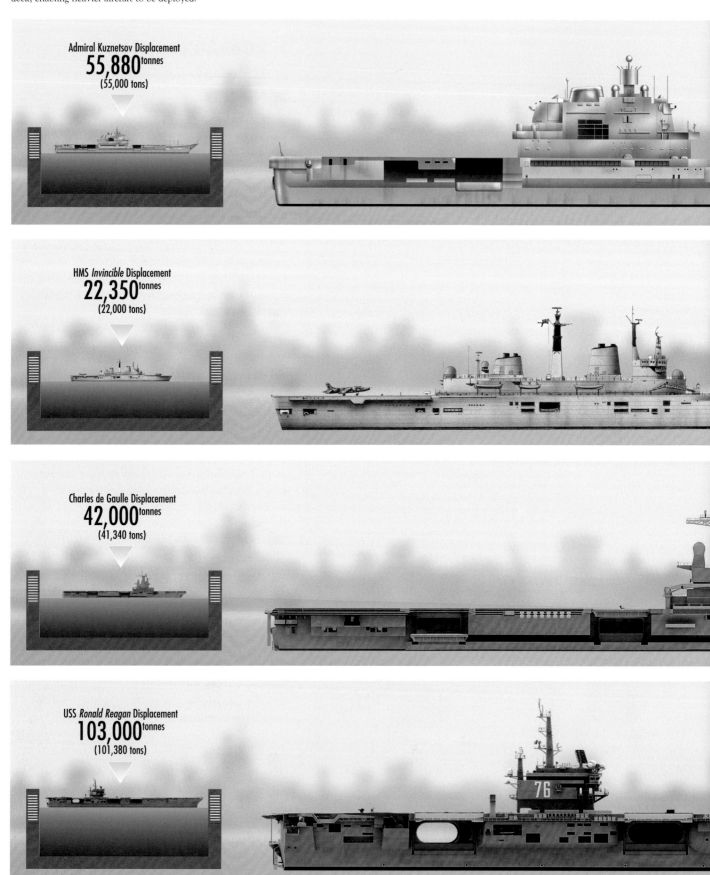

Admiral Kuznetsov Displacement
55,880 tonnes
(55,000 tons)

HMS *Invincible* Displacement
22,350 tonnes
(22,000 tons)

Charles de Gaulle Displacement
42,000 tonnes
(41,340 tons)

USS *Ronald Reagan* Displacement
103,000 tonnes
(101,380 tons)

CHAPTER 8

Aircraft Carriers 1

Full-load Displacement and Missile Launchers

▶ **Admiral Kuznetsov**
▶ **HMS** *Invincible*
▶ **Charles de Gaulle**
▶ **USS** *Ronald Reagan*

Armament

An aircraft carrier should never need to engage any threat directly. Anti-aircraft armament is carried in case the unexpected happens or in case the escorts are swamped by a saturation missile or air attack.

Admiral Kuznetsov
8

Invincible
Goalkeeper CIWS
3

Charles de Gaulle
Sylver launchers
4

USS *Ronald Reagan*
2 x Mk 29 ESSM launchers;
2 x RIM-116 RAM launchers
4

Aircraft carriers exist to provide a mobile base for their air group, and are optimized for that purpose alone. Aircraft carriers are the modern "capital ship," and are as much a status symbol as they are a military asset. A navy with air power, however minor, is a major player in world events and has a significant advantage over a force that must rely on surface vessels and shore-based aircraft.

A carrier relies on its aircraft to deal with submarines and surface craft. It is unlikely that a carrier would be unescorted, and normally the escorts would deal with any threat that slipped past the carrier's air patrols. In the event of an air attack getting right through, the carrier itself relies on decoys and electronic countermeasures to defend against missiles and can engage aircraft with its own weapons. Typically these are short- to medium-range missiles and a CIWS, which is usually a rapid-fire gun in the 20–30mm (0.79–1.2in) range, although the US RIM-116 Rolling Airframe Missile system fulfils the same function.

RIGHT: Aircraft carriers are to an extent the standard by which a navy is judged. Those that can deploy carriers have a higher status than those that do not. This can have far-reaching implications; a navy is a political tool in peacetime as well as a warfighting asset.

Aircraft Carriers 2

Number of Aircraft

- ▶ **Admiral Kuznetsov**
- ▶ **HMS *Invincible***
- ▶ **Charles de Gaulle**
- ▶ **USS *Ronald Reagan***

A carrier's effectiveness is judged to a great extent by the size of its air group. More aircraft mean more sorties can be generated and operations can be sustained despite losses. However, the size of the air group is not the only factor. The efficiency with which it is operated is important; it is worth sacrificing a few aircraft for space to maintain and rearm the air group more efficiently.

The type of aircraft operated is also important. Many small carriers can employ only light aircraft, which lack the range and payload of more powerful planes. The Harrier and its derivatives make ideal aircraft for smaller carriers, as their vectored thrust allows a short take-off and a vertical landing, which does away with the need for catapults and arrester gear. A new generation of vectored-thrust aircraft is beginning to appear, ensuring that the small carrier remains viable.

A large carrier can carry a wide range of planes. A US supercarrier can deploy airborne early warning (AEW) aircraft, plus strike and anti-submarine platforms, and retain a powerful fighter force. Smaller carriers must either carry a few aircraft for each mission or swap between roles by replacing part of their air group. The use of multi-role jets does offset this problem to an extent, but a large carrier's air group remains more efficient in its specialist areas as well as being more numerous.

BELOW: US supercarriers each carry an air group equivalent to some nations' air forces and can operate more or less indefinitely, limited only by aviation fuel and munitions, and by the crew's endurance.

USS *Ronald Reagan*
90 aircraft

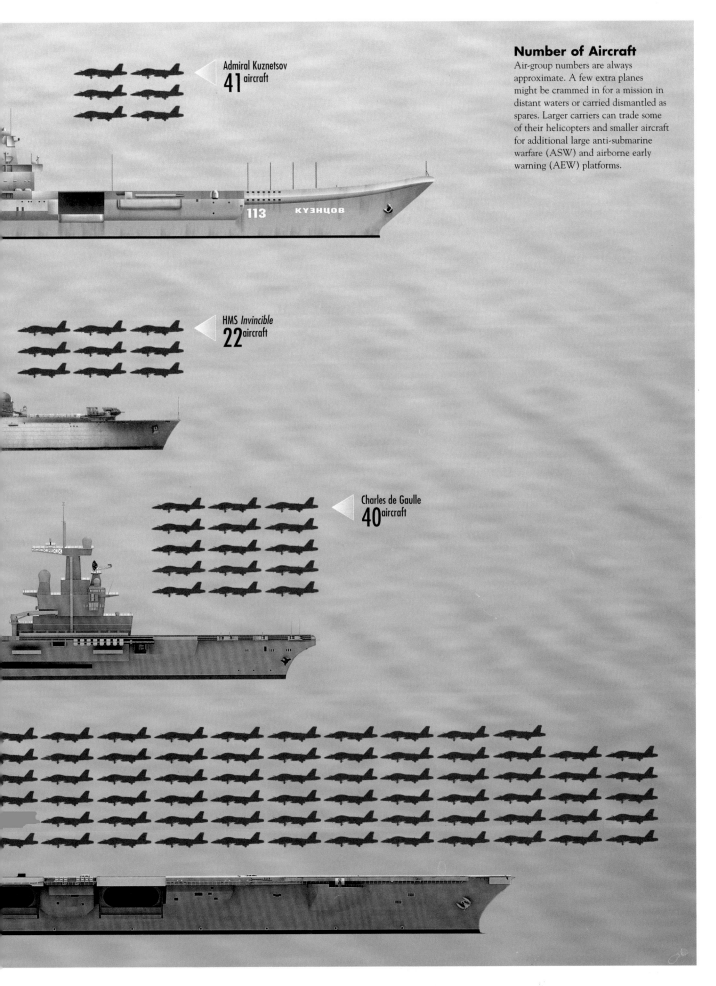

Admiral Kuznetsov
41 aircraft

КУЗНЦОВ
113

Number of Aircraft
Air-group numbers are always approximate. A few extra planes might be crammed in for a mission in distant waters or carried dismantled as spares. Larger carriers can trade some of their helicopters and smaller aircraft for additional large anti-submarine warfare (ASW) and airborne early warning (AEW) platforms.

HMS *Invincible*
22 aircraft

Charles de Gaulle
40 aircraft

CHAPTER 10

Littoral Operations Vessels

Complement, Speed and Displacement

▶ **USS** *Independence*
▶ **USS** *Freedom*
▶ **HDMS** *Esbern Snare*
  (Absalon Class)

For much of the twentieth century, the navies of the major world powers were primarily concerned with "blue-water" operations, i.e. in the open seas. However, there has been a shift towards littoral, or "brown-water," operations in recent years. This requires a different approach to ship design as vessels must operate in relatively shallow and restricted waters close to the sea/land interface and thus within reach of land-based weapons. A blue-water task force has a lot of ocean to move around in, creating ambiguity about its location, but a vessel close inshore is much easier to locate – and what can be located, can be attacked.

Blue-water vessels are primarily concerned with threats from other ships, submarines and aircraft, but the range of threats in the littoral is much greater. So is the range of missions that must be carried out: littoral operations may include bombardment of shore targets or the projection of power inland. To meet these new requirements, the US Navy has created two new designs of warship optimized for brown-water operations. The Freedom class is fairly conventional, while the Independence class uses an advanced trimaran design.

The Danish Absalon class flexible support ships are larger vessels, of conventional hull design, which includes a modular section to allow them to be tailored to different missions. The vessels can act as small landing ships (each can carry a force of 200 troops) or as task-force command vessels. They can also act as support ships, carrying cargo or supplies.

Displacement

In order to achieve maximum flexibility on a limited displacement, vessels of this type often use a modular system which allows unnecessary systems to be replaced with those optimized for the current mission. However, the vessel itself remains a fast and well-armed platform capable of dealing with the whole range of threats that might be encountered in the littoral.

Complement

Vessels of this type have a core crew that is required to operate the vessel, plus a variable number of additional personnel depending on the mission. These can include troops, humanitarian-aid workers or aircrews. The vessel can be quickly retasked by changing these personnel and their equipment, with the core crew remaining constant.

USS *Independence* Complement
40men

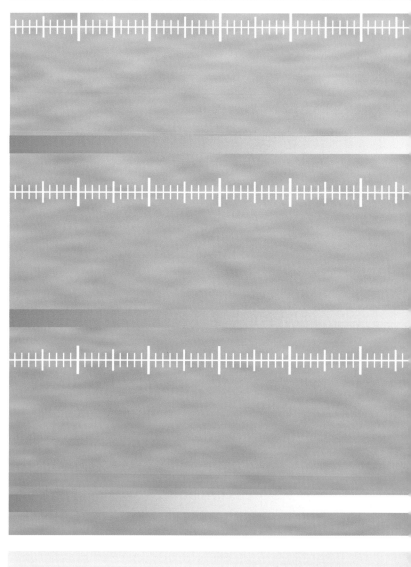

USS *Independence* Displacement
2829tonnes
(2784 tons)

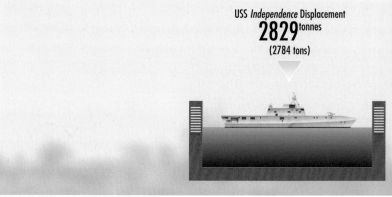

USS *Freedom* Complement
50men

HDMS *Esbern Snare*
100men

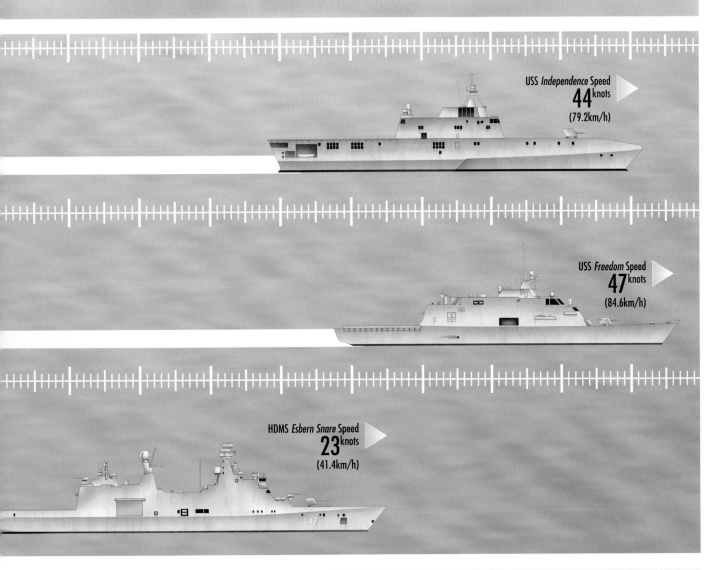

USS *Independence* Speed
44knots
(79.2km/h)

USS *Freedom* Speed
47knots
(84.6km/h)

HDMS *Esbern Snare* Speed
23knots
(41.4km/h)

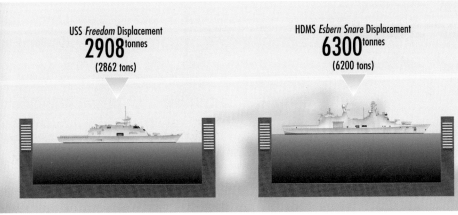

USS *Freedom* Displacement
2908tonnes
(2862 tons)

HDMS *Esbern Snare* Displacement
6300tonnes
(6200 tons)

Number of Aircraft

Vessels of this type are sometimes mistaken for aircraft carriers, but their role is quite different. Some classes can and do operate fixed-wing aircraft, notably the AV-8B Harrier, but it is helicopters that provide the vessels' main power-projection capability.

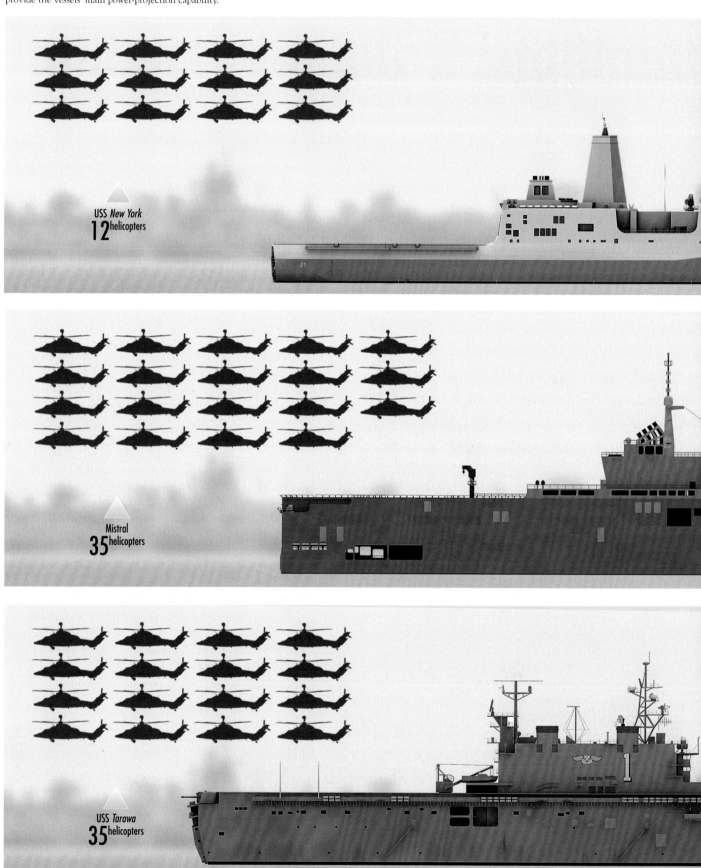

USS *New York*
12 helicopters

Mistral
35 helicopters

USS *Tarawa*
35 helicopters

CHAPTER 11

Landing Ships and Support Ships

Number of Helicopters

▶ **USS *New York***
▶ **Mistral**
▶ **USS *Tarawa***

The ability to project power ashore is a vital part of maritime strategy. For centuries, this meant landing troops onto a beach, which might be heavily defended, and then pushing inland towards the final objective. Helicopter-carrying landing ships make it possible to strike directly at inland targets, bypassing beach defenses and other obstacles, though assault craft can also be used where it is desirable to establish a presence ashore. One advantage to using landing ships in this way is the ability to move up and down an enemy coast, striking where necessary from the safety of a task force held offshore and out of reach of retaliation by enemy ground forces.

Helicopters are the critical component of such operations. They are the link between the landing ship and the troops ashore, ferrying combat and support personnel, casualties, supplies and ammunition to and from the area of operations, and in many cases act as mobile fire support as well. Thus, although landing ships are armed for self-defense, it is their troops and helicopters which are their primary combat system.

BELOW: The French Mistral class was designed as an "intervention ship," capable of dealing with situations ranging from a war to a natural disaster. The ship provides a mobile but secure base from which to stage operations ashore and is equipped to carry out a range of humanitarian and military missions.

CHAPTER 12

Nuclear Attack Subs

Speed and Number of Torpedo Tubes

▶ "Granei" Class
▶ Barracuda Class
▶ Seawolf Class
▶ "Shang" Class
▶ Virginia Class

Nuclear propulsion enabled the submarine to become a true underwater vessel, capable of remaining submerged for weeks at a time. Previously, submarines functioned more as surface vessels that could submerge for a time, using battery power to move relatively slowly underwater and returning to the surface to recharge the batteries using air-dependent diesel engines. The hull form of these early boats reflects their essentially surface-craft nature, while that of the modern submarine is optimized for underwater operations.

Early submarines needed large numbers of tubes to launch a spread of unguided torpedoes. This made hits more likely, and ensured that if one torpedo malfunctioned, the attack would not necessarily be wasted. Modern boats, using guided torpedoes, do not need so many tubes. However, a certain degree of redundancy is important in a combat vessel, and the ability to simultaneously attack more than one target requires multiple tubes. This also allows the boat to hold some tubes ready to fire in self-defense while others are being reloaded.

BELOW: The Astute class is the latest Royal Navy attack-submarine design. In addition to advanced torpedoes, the Astute class can carry Tomahawk cruise missiles, which enable it to project power far inland. However, submarines remain primarily maritime-warfare platforms.

Speed

Speed is important to an attack submarine, both in terms of covering the great distances between home port and patrol area and when in contact with the enemy. High speed produces a lot of noise, largely from cavitation – i.e. bubbles are caused by the propeller's motion through the water; they then collapse, making noise that can betray the submarine's position. The deeper a submarine dives, the faster it can go without cavitating, so fast transits are usually made at great depth.

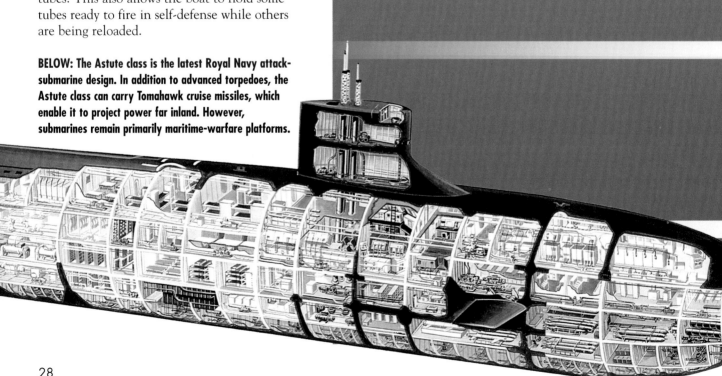

Torpedo tubes are used by some boats to deliver underwater-launched missiles, not to mention divers, as well as torpedoes. Missile capability allows an attack submarine to make stand-off strikes on shipping and to attack targets far inshore, often with complete surprise.

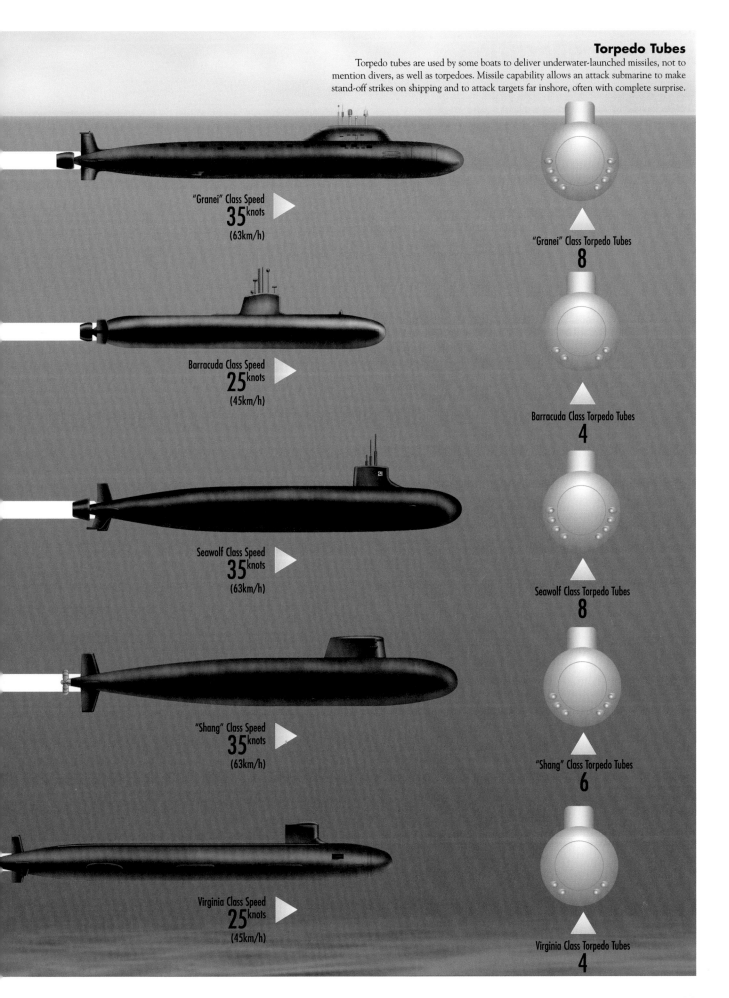

"Granei" Class Speed
35knots
(63km/h)

"Granei" Class Torpedo Tubes
8

Barracuda Class Speed
25knots
(45km/h)

Barracuda Class Torpedo Tubes
4

Seawolf Class Speed
35knots
(63km/h)

Seawolf Class Torpedo Tubes
8

"Shang" Class Speed
35knots
(63km/h)

"Shang" Class Torpedo Tubes
6

Virginia Class Speed
25knots
(45km/h)

Virginia Class Torpedo Tubes
4

CHAPTER 13

Fourth-generation Nuclear Submarines

Speed and Depth

▶ "Granei" Class
▶ Seawolf Class
▶ Virginia Class

Attack submarines have matured from purely anti-shipping vessels into multi-role platforms that can engage targets above or below the surface, or even on land. In turn, they can be attacked by surface vessels, submarines and aircraft as well as passive weapons such as mines. In order to make a successful attack and withdraw afterwards, the boat needs to make as little noise as possible. A deep-diving sub is more difficult to detect with sonar due to temperature layers in the water.

High underwater speeds can cause a great deal of noise due to water turbulence around the boat and cavitation caused by the propeller blades. The extreme water pressures at great depths enable a boat to run faster without cavitating, so the ability to dive deep allows a higher speed to be maintained without compromising stealth. Another way to reduce propeller noise is to use pump-jet propulsion, such as is employed in the Virginia class.

The Russian "Granei" class and the US Virginia class have vertical-launch tubes for their cruise missiles, enabling a full missile load to be carried without reducing the available torpedo armament. Conversely, the Seawolf class can carry a mix of up to 50 cruise missiles, anti-ship missiles and torpedoes, varying the loadout according to the needs of the mission. The Seawolf class was developed during the Cold War as a top-end weapons system intended to gain supremacy at sea. In the post–Cold War environment its cost was seen as excessive, and the cheaper Virginia class was put into production instead.

Seawolf Class Depth
610ᵐ
(2001ft)

LEFT: The Seawolf class has eight torpedo tubes to the four of the Virginia class and uses these to launch all of its weapons.

Depth

Although the depths that a modern attack sub can dive to are impressive, it is only possible to reach the bottom in relatively shallow water such as around the continental shelf. A boat that goes too deep will suffer structural failure and be lost.

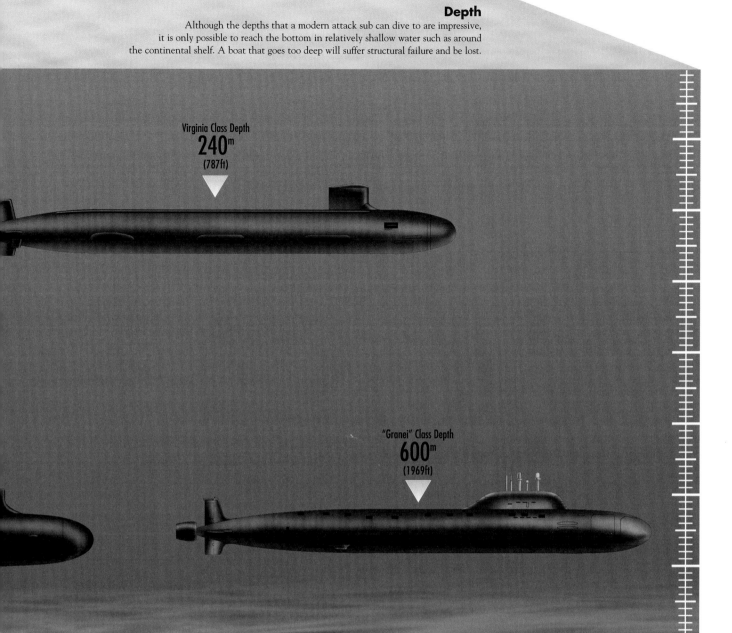

Virginia Class Depth
240m
(787ft)

"Granei" Class Depth
600m
(1969ft)

Speed

Extremes of speed are only used in an emergency, and then generally when running at great depth. Although a 35-knot (63km/h) submarine may be able to stay ahead of pursuing surface ships, it cannot outrun helicopters and aircraft. At some point, the boat must slow down and hope its pursuers lose the contact.

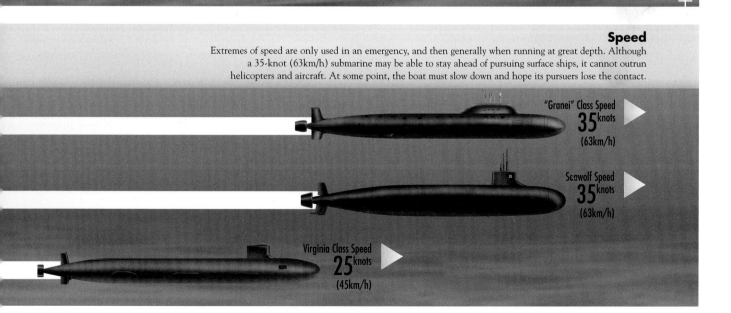

"Granei" Class Speed
35knots
(63km/h)

Seawolf Speed
35knots
(63km/h)

Virginia Class Speed
25knots
(45km/h)

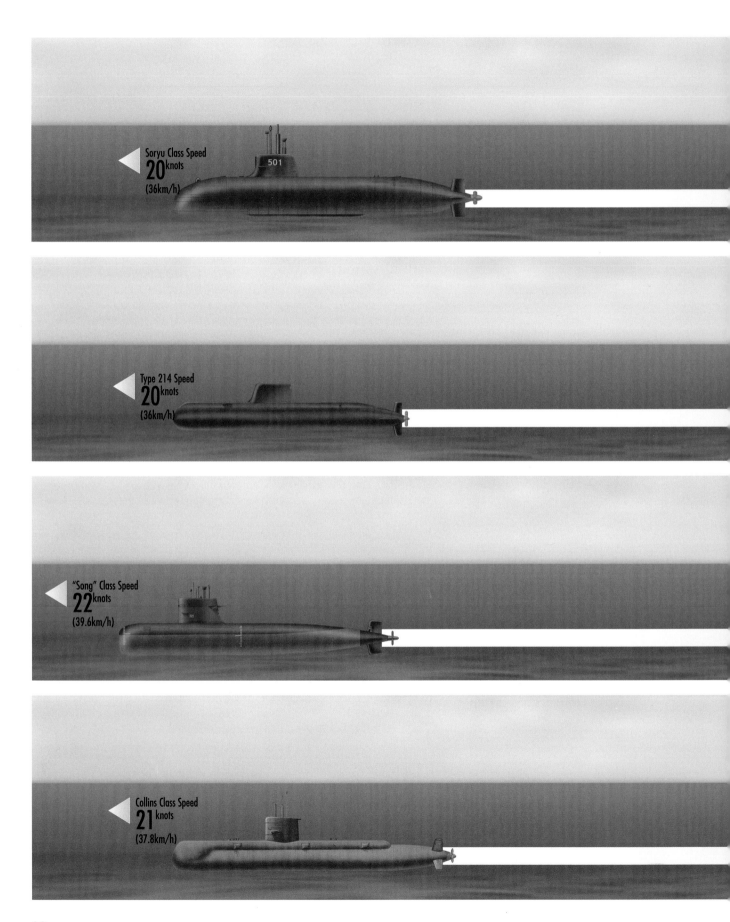

Soryu Class Speed
20knots
(36km/h)

Type 214 Speed
20knots
(36km/h)

"Song" Class Speed
22knots
(39.6km/h)

Collins Class Speed
21knots
(37.8km/h)

CHAPTER 14

Conventional Attack Submarines 1

Surface and Submerged Speed

▶ **Soryu Class**
▶ **Type 214**
▶ **"Song" Class**
▶ **Collins Class**

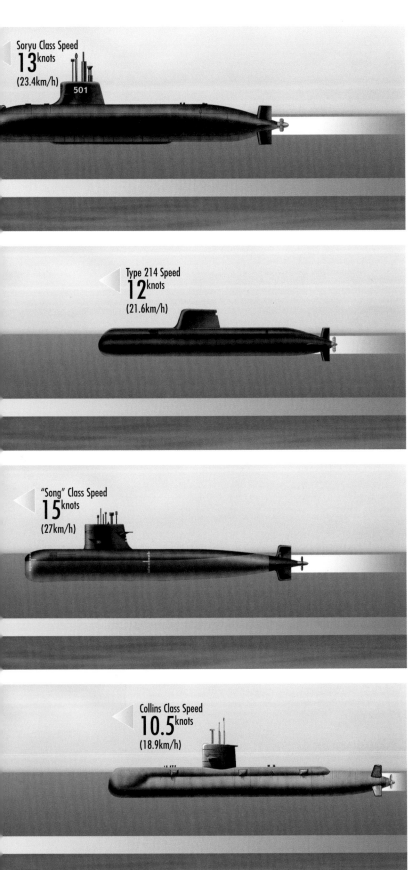

Soryu Class Speed
13knots
(23.4km/h)

Type 214 Speed
12knots
(21.6km/h)

"Song" Class Speed
15knots
(27km/h)

Collins Class Speed
10.5knots
(18.9km/h)

Early submersibles used a boat-shaped hull and were significantly faster on the surface than underwater. This was a key factor in the convoy battles of World War II. A submarine that was forced down by escorts, even if it was not critically damaged or sunk, could not keep up with a convoy and would lose touch. However, modern submarines are designed primarily for underwater operations and are much faster when fully submerged.

Whereas a nuclear-powered boat can maintain high speed for as long as its reactor is functioning, a conventional vessel must conserve fuel even when on the surface or using a snorkel. Modern air-independent propulsion systems greatly increase the underwater endurance of a boat; even so, high speed can only be maintained for a finite period.

Modern boats typically use a whale-shaped or teardrop-shaped hull, which gives good resistance to water pressure as well as improving the flow of water over the hull. Streamlining is also important for noise reduction. A hull with many angles and projections creates eddies which will slow the boat down and produce underwater noise, which becomes much more pronounced when the boat is moving fast.

Noise is the submarine's worst enemy, as it allows a hostile vessel to detect and track the boat and also interferes with its own passive sensors. A submarine transiting fast underwater can become "blind and deaf" due to self-noise, and at the same time advertises its presence to any vessel using passive sonar detection.

Speed

Conventional attack submarines are sufficiently desirable that they are a viable export item. The Scorpène class and Type 214 designs have achieved considerable overseas sales success, while the "Song" class (Type 039) has been offered to Thailand and Pakistan. The Collins class was custom designed for a single operator and has not been offered for export.

CHAPTER 15

Conventional Attack Submarines 2

Number of Torpedo Tubes

▶ **Soryu Class**
▶ **Type 214**
▶ **"Song" Class**
▶ **Collins Class**

Not all navies have the capability, or the desire, to operate nuclear attack submarines. Some prefer to have nothing to do with nuclear energy, some lack the technical ability to maintain and operate a reactor, and others simply prefer to rely on conventional vessels. Although modern diesel-electric submarines are still dependent on air from the atmosphere, the invention of the snorkel in World War II enabled a conventional boat to stay down for an extended period, drawing in air while remaining submerged. Recent advances in air-independent propulsion (AIP) have also increased the viability of non-nuclear submarines.

Although their diesel-electric propulsion systems are not very different from those of previous generations, today's conventional attack submarines are vastly more capable than their predecessors. Their torpedo tubes can be used to deliver torpedoes and missiles, and many classes of boat can also lay mines. The main advantage of submarine-laid mines is stealth. Minefields can be laid defensively, to protect friendly installations, or as part of sea-denial operations. It is even possible to lay a minefield offensively, close to an enemy port or in an area that hostiles are likely to pass through or operate in.

The exact mix of weapons carried by a given boat depends upon the mission at hand. With a full load of torpedoes, the Chinese "Song" class can carry 18 weapons, though some would probably be swapped for missiles under most circumstances, granting the capability to attack a variety of targets.

LEFT: The Collins class consists of six diesel-electric submarines built and operated by the Royal Australian Navy (RAN).

Soryu Class Torpedo Tubes
6

Type 214 Torpedo Tubes
4

"Song" Class Torpedo Tubes
6

Collins Class Torpedo Tubes
6

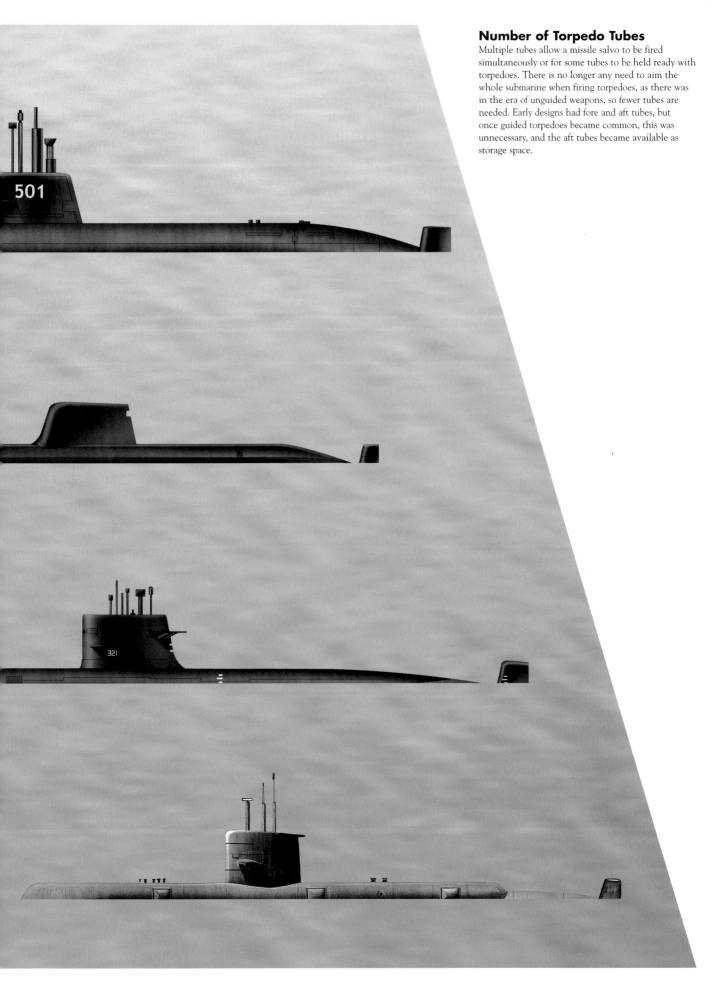

CHAPTER 16

Patrol Submarines Head to Head

Submerged Speed, Number of Torpedo Tubes, Surface Range

▶ **Walrus Class**
▶ **Scorpène Class**

Conventional (i.e. non-nuclear-powered) attack submarines are an important part of many national navies and can be highly effective in the hands of a well-trained crew. Conventional attack submarines lack the all-but-unlimited range of nuclear boats but are still capable of extended patrols. Underwater endurance is limited, but air-independent propulsion (AIP) systems and advanced battery technology permit modern boats to operate underwater for far longer than previous generations. In addition to endurance, the primary difference between nuclear and non-nuclear boats is sustained underwater speed. A nuclear boat can maintain a higher speed than one that must depend on batteries.

Nuclear power was originally considered for the Dutch Walrus class, but conventional diesel-electric propulsion was finally settled upon for technical as well as financial reasons. The resulting vessel is very quiet underwater and can deliver a range of weapons. The Walrus class is equipped for a torpedo or missile attack against a variety of targets, using guided 533mm (21in) torpedoes or Sub-Harpoon missiles.

The Scorpène class was a joint French–Spanish project that has thus far achieved sales to Chile, India and Brazil. Primary armament is guided torpedoes, launched from six tubes, compared with four in the Walrus class. The Scorpène can launch Exocet missiles, which have a shorter effective range than Harpoon, but is also equipped for mine laying operations. Flexibility is important to many potential operators, as a relatively small naval budget does not permit several specialist vessels to be purchased.

Submarines are effective ship-killers, but they can carry out a number of other roles, including reconnaissance and intelligence-gathering. The possession of a credible submarine force is seen in some quarters as a symbol of a "serious navy" that can exert significant influence over the waters to which it is deployed.

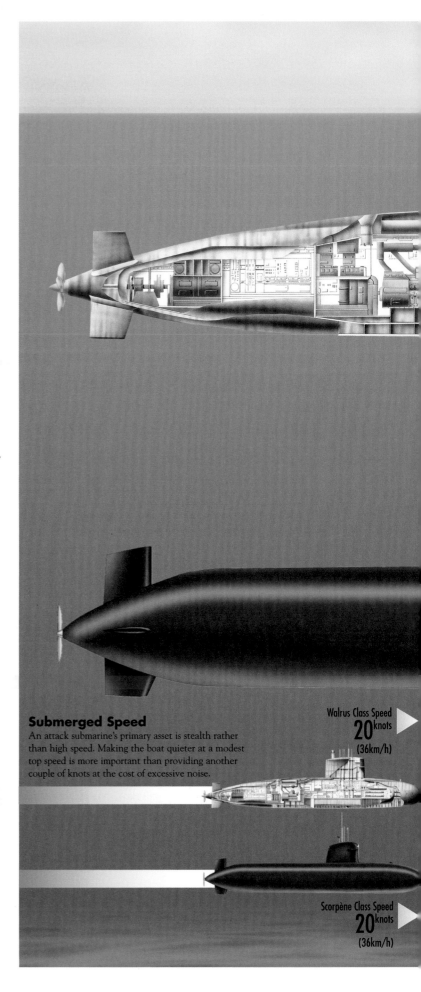

Submerged Speed
An attack submarine's primary asset is stealth rather than high speed. Making the boat quieter at a modest top speed is more important than providing another couple of knots at the cost of excessive noise.

Walrus Class Speed
20 knots
(36km/h)

Scorpène Class Speed
20 knots
(36km/h)

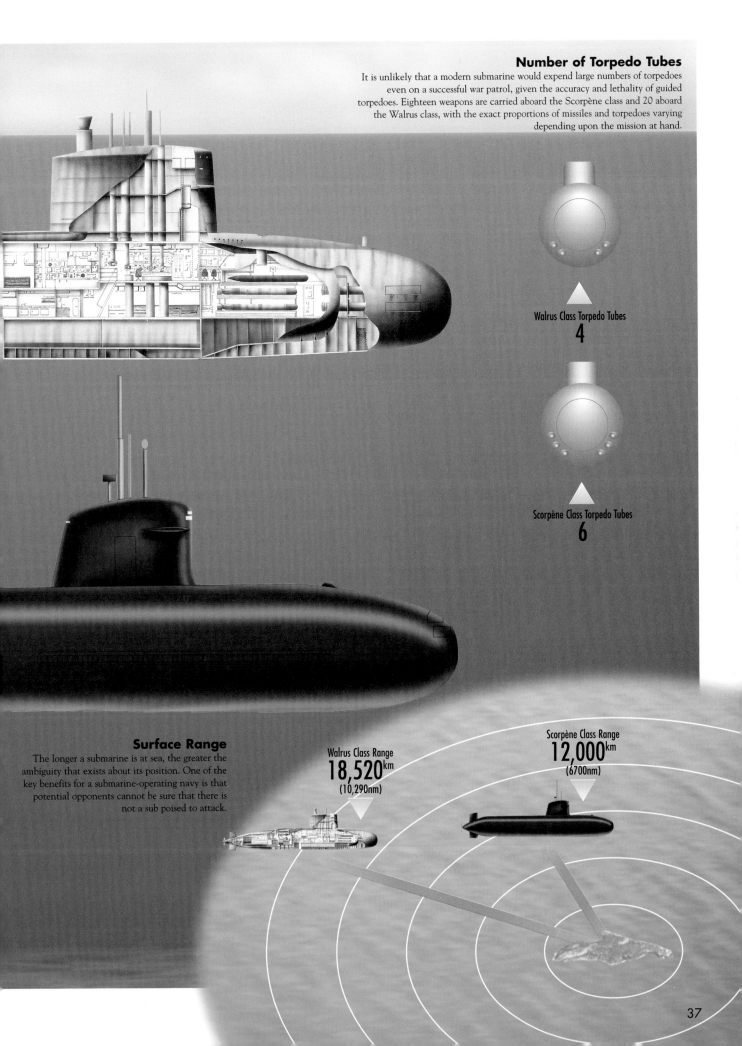

Number of Torpedo Tubes

It is unlikely that a modern submarine would expend large numbers of torpedoes even on a successful war patrol, given the accuracy and lethality of guided torpedoes. Eighteen weapons are carried aboard the Scorpène class and 20 aboard the Walrus class, with the exact proportions of missiles and torpedoes varying depending upon the mission at hand.

Walrus Class Torpedo Tubes
4

Scorpène Class Torpedo Tubes
6

Surface Range

The longer a submarine is at sea, the greater the ambiguity that exists about its position. One of the key benefits for a submarine-operating navy is that potential opponents cannot be sure that there is not a sub poised to attack.

Walrus Class Range
18,520km
(10,290nm)

Scorpène Class Range
12,000km
(6700nm)

Number of Missiles

To be a credible deterrent or an effective warfighting asset, a ballistic-missile submarine must carry a significant number of missiles. The ability to visit massive devastation on a hostile nation is a key part of the boat's deterrent role – a handful of missiles may not be a grave enough threat.

CHAPTER 17

Missile Submarines

Number of Missiles

▶ **Ohio Class**
▶ **"Borei" Class**
▶ **INS Arihant**
▶ **Triomphant Class**
▶ **Vanguard Class**

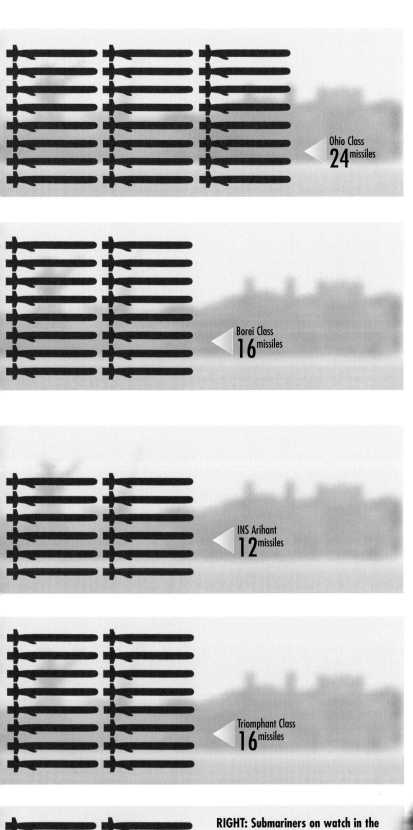

Ohio Class
24 missiles

Borei Class
16 missiles

INS Arihant
12 missiles

Triomphant Class
16 missiles

Vanguard Class
16 missiles

Traditionally, all submarines are "boats" and not "ships"; even those with the power to sink any vessel and destroy whole cities with a missile strike. However, these boats are a critical component in both peacetime and wartime strategy. To some extent their existence is a factor in preventing conflicts "going nuclear," making them a powerful force for peace and stability.

If the worst happens and an all-out nuclear exchange begins, missile-submarine bases are a key target and in any case the matter will be decided long before a distant boat can return to port to rearm. Thus in a nuclear conflict, "boomers," as ballistic-missile boats are popularly tagged, will fight with what they have. Once a boat's strategic missiles are expended, it might be able to contribute as a reconnaissance or anti-shipping platform, but a second salvo of ballistic missiles is not likely to be an option.

Some ballistic-missile submarines can launch cruise missiles in addition to their ballistic weapons or can be converted to carry them instead. The Ohio class has been modified to carry large numbers of vertically launched cruise missiles in place of its strategic missiles, enabling it to carry out a conventional stand-off anti-shipping or land-attack mission.

RIGHT: Submariners on watch in the control area of a nuclear submarine.

Chapter 18

Submarine-launched Torpedoes

Range and Warhead Weight

▶ **DTCN L5**
▶ **DTCN F17**
▶ **FFV Tp42 Series**
▶ **Spearfish**

Torpedoes come in two general types, known as heavy and light. Both are guided, but differ in their mode of attack. Lightweight torpedoes carry a relatively small warhead and are designed to impact a target directly, detonating on contact. They are usually self-guided, using acoustic homing, and are primarily anti-submarine weapons. Lightweight torpedoes are generally deployed by surface vessels, helicopters and aircraft as well as submarines, whereas heavyweight torpedoes are primarily submarine-launched weapons. Only a few nations use heavyweight torpedoes from any platform other than submarines.

The heavyweight torpedo has a much larger warhead than lightweight versions and ideally is detonated directly beneath the keel of a target vessel. The exploding warhead creates a bubble of gas, which lifts up the central section of the ship. The target vessel's own weight places incredible strain on its structure as this occurs, possibly resulting in a "broken back" and rapid sinking. Even a more distant detonation can cause severe damage due to underwater shock.

Heavyweight torpedoes frequently use wire-guidance, receiving signals from the launching submarine for the approach to the target and switching to active sonar for terminal guidance. Attacks can be made from very long ranges using guided weapons, which greatly improves a sub's survivability. However, a long-range attack means that the torpedo will be in the water for an extended period, during which the target could move out of range. High speed and long-duration propulsion are important if a fast-moving target is to be caught and successfully attacked.

Lightweight torpedoes are standardized in many countries at a diameter of 324mm (12.8in), and heavyweight torpedoes at 533mm (21in). Russia uses 650mm (25.6in) torpedoes for some tasks, while Sweden has 400mm (15.7in) weapons that represent a compromise between heavy and light torpedoes and are capable of a range of missions.

Range

Although torpedoes have a long maximum range, launching from close to the target reduces the chance of successful evasion or other countermeasures. Spearfish and some other torpedoes can be used in short-range mode, trading stand-off capability for very high underwater speed by burning rapidly through the available propellant.

Warhead Weight

Torpedoes intended for direct impact tend to use a small shaped-charge warhead focused into the target. Heavyweight torpedoes have traditionally relied on the gas-bubble effect, but future weapons may use multi-mode warheads capable of directional detonation when necessary.

DTCN L5 Warhead Weight: 150kg (331lb)

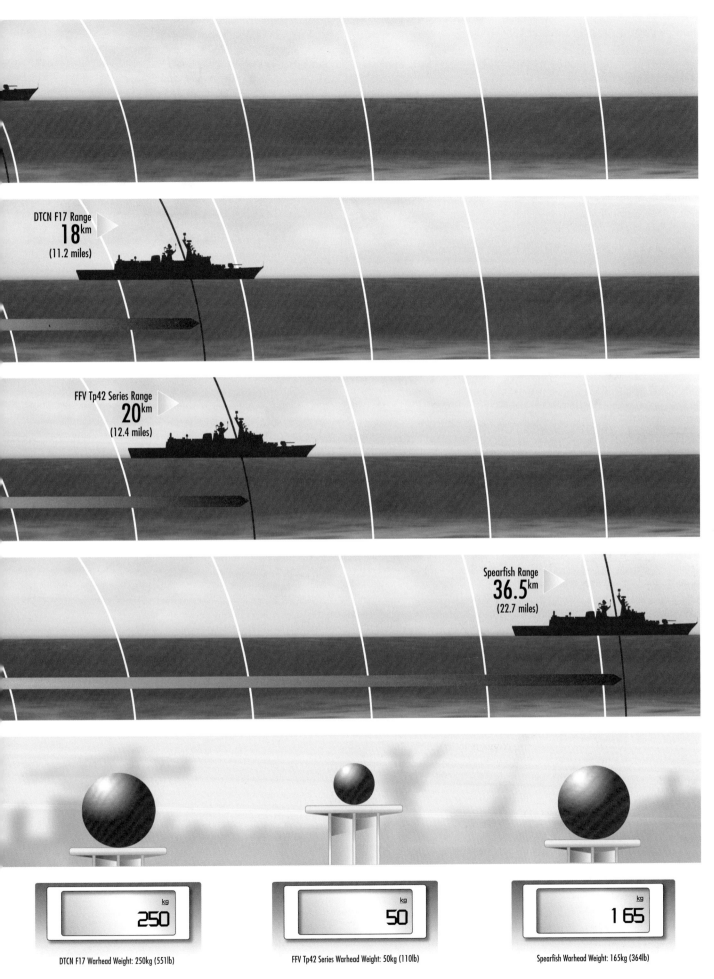

DTCN F17 Range
18km
(11.2 miles)

FFV Tp42 Series Range
20km
(12.4 miles)

Spearfish Range
36.5km
(22.7 miles)

kg
250

kg
50

kg
165

DTCN F17 Warhead Weight: 250kg (551lb)

FFV Tp42 Series Warhead Weight: 50kg (110lb)

Spearfish Warhead Weight: 165kg (364lb)

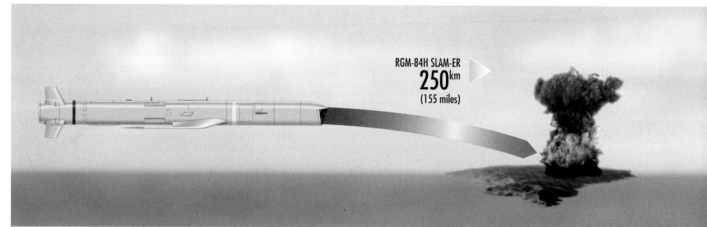

RGM-84H SLAM-ER
250km
(155 miles)

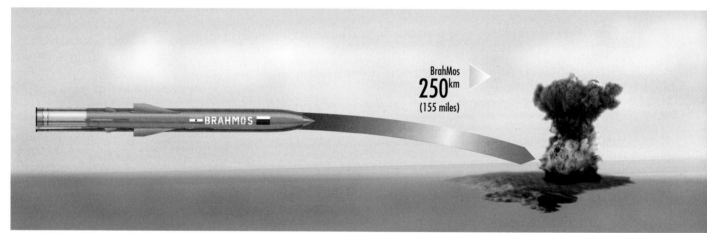

BrahMos
250km
(155 miles)

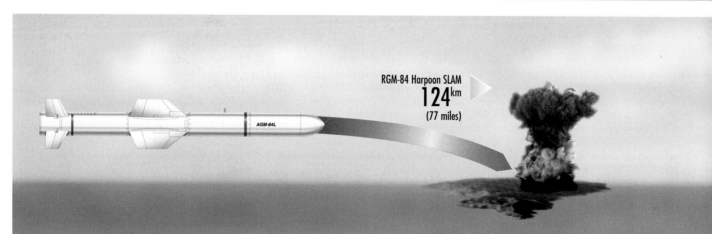

RGM-84 Harpoon SLAM
124km
(77 miles)

CHAPTER 19

Land Attack Missiles

Range

Tomahawk
1700km
(1056 miles)

▶ **RGM-84 Harpoon SLAM**
▶ **RGM-84H SLAM-ER**
▶ **BrahMos**
▶ **Tomahawk**

Range

The key to effective land attack missiles is a combination of long range and good guidance systems. GPS or inertial guidance can be used. Terrain-mapping radar is also an option, though there are not many terrain features in the sea to provide guidance updates, so this is primarily useful once the coast has been crossed. Terminal guidance may use thermal, radar or optical systems to seek a specific target or rely on GPS to hit a pre-programmed area.

Shore bombardment has always been an important naval mission, but until quite recently most targets were out of range of naval weapons. The advent of the long-range missile changed that, and, in recent conflicts, it has been possible to attack targets far inland using missiles launched from ships and submarines. A surface task force located offshore may be beyond the range of effective retaliation, or could move into range, attack and then retire to a safe distance. Submarine-launched land attack missiles take this one stage further; the target nation might not even be aware that a threat is present until the missiles strike.

The Tomahawk missile was developed as a nuclear delivery system but has matured into an extremely long-range conventional missile that uses GPS, terrain-matching and inertial guidance. The recent Tactical Tomahawk variant has been redesigned to take targeting updates from sensors mounted on other platforms such as aircraft, UAVs (unmanned aerial vehicles) and personnel on the ground. The Indian BrahMos missile has a vastly shorter range but is much faster, improving the missile's ability to penetrate enemy defenses.

LEFT: The Harpoon anti-ship missile was developed into Harpoon SLAM (Standoff Land Attack Missile) by incorporating a GPS guidance unit plus systems from the Walleye and Maverick missiles. Further upgrades created SLAM-ER (Expanded Response).

CHAPTER 20

Submarine-launched ICBMs

Range and Warhead Weight

▶ **Polaris A3**
▶ **SS-N-18 "Stingray" (RSM-50)**
▶ **SS-N-20 "Sturgeon" (RSM-52)**

In the early days of ballistic-missile technology, weapons had a very short range and had to be carried close to the target country. A submarine provided an effective means of doing so, provoking extensive efforts to counter the threat with anti-submarine aircraft and surface patrols. As missile ranges have increased, it has become possible to attack targets deep within a continent from distant reaches of the ocean, enormously complicating the problem of preventing an attack.

Nuclear missiles carried aboard a "boomer," which could be literally anywhere in the world's oceans, providing an effective deterrent to nuclear attack. A hostile nation might conceivably get lucky and locate a boomer with an attack submarine, but the probability is vanishingly small. Thus the submarine-borne missiles are almost certain to survive a first strike intended to wipe out land-based missile and bomber bases. Even if such a strike succeeded, which is by no means guaranteed, retaliation would be inevitable.

Most nations that operate nuclear missile submarines defend them by sending the vessels on long patrols into remote areas, relying on concealment to protect the boats. The Russian approach was rather different: missile submarines were assigned to "bastions," which were sea areas protected by air, surface and submarine patrols. Although the general location of the boats was obvious, attack by ballistic missile remained impractical, and the bastions were very heavily defended against incursion by attack submarines. Both methods served the same purpose: to ensure that a first strike by the enemy was pointless and therefore unlikely to be considered.

Range

Modern sea-launched strategic missiles have an extremely long range, greatly reducing the time required to redeploy boats against a new threat. The very fact that a boomer could be, and probably is, in range is a powerful deterrent to any nation considering the use of nuclear weapons.

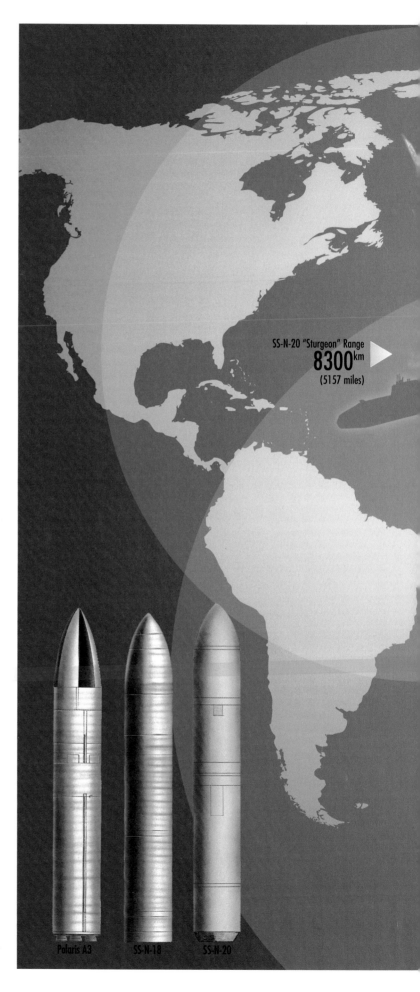

SS-N-20 "Sturgeon" Range
8300km
(5157 miles)

Polaris A3   SS-N-18   SS-N-20

Polaris A3 Range
4748km
(2950 miles)

SS-N-18 "Stingray" Range
8000km
(4971 miles)

Warhead Weight

Multiple warheads enable a single missile to attack more than
one target or to cause more damage to a single dispersed target,
such as a city, than a single, larger, explosion. A pattern of
shockwaves is far more effective at cracking hardened targets,
like missile silos, than a single detonation.

KT
1 000₁₀₀kT x10

KT
1 400200kT x7

KT
1 8060kT x3

SS_N-20 Sturgeon

SS_N-18 (RSM-50) Stingray

Polaris A3

Glossary

aircraft carrier A warship with a flight deck on which aircraft can be launched and landed.

armament Weapons, arms; a military or naval force.

asset Something useful in an effort to foil or defeat an enemy; a piece of military equipment; an advantage or resource; an item of value that is owned.

combatant One who is engaged or ready to engage in combat.

corvette A highly maneuverable armed escort ship that is smaller than a destroyer.

countermeasure An action or device designed to negate or offset another; a military system or device intended to thwart a sensing mechanism (as radar).

decoy Someone or something used to lure or lead another into a trap; someone or something used to draw attention away from another.

deploy To place in battle formation or appropriate positions; to spread out, utilize or arrange for a deliberate purpose.

destroyer A small fast warship used especially to support larger vessels and usually armed with guns, depth charges, torpedoes and often guided missiles.

deterrent Serving to discourage, turn away from or prevent an unwanted action or outcome.

displacement The volume or weight of a fluid (as water) displaced by a floating body (as a ship) of equal weight.

electronic countermeasure The disruption of the operation of an enemy's equipment (as by jamming radio or radar signals).

escort A protective screen of warships or fighter planes or a single ship or plane used to fend off enemy attack from one or more vulnerable craft; accompaniment by a person or an armed protector (as a ship).

frigate A modern warship that is smaller than a destroyer.

hull The frame or body of a ship or boat exclusive of masts, yards, sails and rigging; the main body of a usually large or heavy craft or vehicle (as an airship or tank).

innovative Characterized by the introduction of new ideas, methods or devices.

missile An object (as a weapon) thrown or projected usually so as to strike something at a distance.

nautical mile (knot) A British unit equal to 6,080 feet (1853.2 meters); an international unit equal to exactly 6,076.115 feet or 1.15 statute miles (1,852 meters), used officially in the United States since July 1, 1954.

patrol A unit of persons or vehicles employed for reconnaissance, security or combat.

radar A device or system consisting usually of a synchronized radio transmitter and receiver that emits radio waves and processes their reflections for display and is used especially for detecting and locating objects (as aircraft) or surface features (as of a planet).

range The horizontal distance to which a projectile can be propelled; the horizontal distance between a weapon and target; the maximum distance a vehicle or craft can travel without refueling.

sensor A device that responds to a physical stimulus (as heat, light, sound, pressure, magnetism or a particular motion) and transmits a resulting impulse (as for measurement or operating a control).

stealth A military design characteristic consisting of oblique angular construction and avoidance of vertical surfaces that is intended to produce a very weak radar return; the act or action of proceeding furtively, secretly or imperceptibly; the state of being furtive or unobtrusive.

vessel A watercraft bigger than a rowboat; a ship.

warhead The section of a missile containing the explosive, chemical or incendiary charge.

For More Information

Coast Guard Museum
U.S. Coast Guard Academy
15 Mohegan Avenue
New London, CT 06320-4195
(860) 444-8511
Web site: http://www.uscg.mil/hq/cg092/museum
On the grounds of the picturesque U. S. Coast Guard Academy, the Coast Guard Museum contains artifacts that span the two hundred year history of America's premier maritime service. Featuring everything from models of a series of early steamships to the 270-foot (82 m) cutter that plies the waters of today, the craftsmanship captures the changes in ship design over the last two hundred years.

Intrepid Sea, Air, and Space Museum
Pier 86

West 46th St and 12th Avenue
New York, NY 10036-4103
(877) 957-SHIP (7447)
Web site: http://www.intrepidmuseum.org
Since 1982, the Intrepid, an actual aircraft carrier, has become both a New York City and an American icon, as well as a museum dedicated to building awareness and understanding of history, science and service through its collections, exhibitions and public and educational programs.

National Museum of the U.S. Navy
Washington Navy Yard
805 Kidder Breese Street SE
Washington, DC 20374-5060
Web site: http://www.history.navy.mil/branches/org8-1.htm
Devoted to the display of naval artifacts, models, documents and fine art, the museum chronicles the history of the United States Navy from the American Revolution to the present conflicts. Interactive exhibits commemorate the Navy's wartime heroes and battles as well as peacetime contributions in exploration, diplomacy, navigation and humanitarian service.

Naval Undersea Museum
Navy Region Northwest
1 Garnett Way Keyport, WA 98345
(360) 396-4148
Web site: http://www.history.navy.mil/museums/keyport/index1.htm
The museum's mission is to preserve, collect and interpret Naval undersea history, science and operations for the benefit of the U.S. Navy and the people of the United States.

U.S. Naval Academy Museum
Preble Hall, 118 Maryland Avenue
Annapolis, MD 21402
(410) 293-2108
Web site: http://www.usna.edu/Museum
Located on the grounds of the U.S. Naval Academy, the museum offers two floors of exhibits about the history of seapower, the development of the U.S. Navy and the role of the U.S. Naval Academy in producing officers capable of leading America's sailors and marines. Its displays combine historical artifacts with video and audio technology to bring to life the stories of the men and women who have served their country at sea.

Web Sites

Due to the changing nature of Internet links, Rosen Publishing has developed an online list of Web sites related to the subject of this book. This site is updated regularly. Please use this link to access the list:

http://www.rosenlinks.com/MODW/Naval

For Further Reading

Grant, R. G. Battle at Sea: 3,000 Years of Naval Warfare. New York, NY: DK Publishing, 2011.
Ireland, Bernard. An Illustrated History of Destroyers of the World. Wigston, England: Anness, 2011.
Leeman, William P. The Long Road to Annapolis: The Founding of the Naval Academy and the Emerging American Republic. Chapel Hill, NC: University of North Carolina Press, 2010.
Molland, Anthony F., ed. The Maritime Engineering Reference Book: A Guide to Ship Design, Construction, and Operation. Burlington, MA: Butterworth-Heinemann, 2008.
Parker, John. The Submarine: An Illustrated History from 1900-1950. Wigston, England: Anness, 2008.
Sayers, Ken W. Uncommon Warriors: 200 Years of the Most Unusual American Naval Vessels. Bethesda, MD: Naval Institute Press, 2012.
Thursfield, James R. Naval Warfare. New York, NY: Cambridge University Press, 2012.
Tillman, Barrett. Enterprise: America's Fightingest Ship and the Men Who Helped Win World War II. New York, NY: Simon & Schuster, 2012.
Toll, Ian W. Pacific Crucible: War at Sea in the Pacific, 1941-1942. New York, NY: W.W. Norton & Co., 2011.

Toll, Ian W. *Six Frigates: The Epic History of the Founding of the U.S. Navy*. New York, NY: W.W. Norton & Co., 2008.

Ujifusa, Steven. *A Man and His Ship: America's Greatest Naval Architect and His Quest to Build the S.S. United States*. New York, NY: Simon & Schuster, 2012.

Woodward, C. Vann. *The Battle for Leyte Gulf: The Incredible Story of World War II's Largest Naval Battle*. New York, NY: Skyhorse Publishing, 2007.

Index

About the Author

Martin J. Dougherty is a writer and editor specializing in military and defense topics. He is an expert on asymmetric and non-conventional warfa[re]. His published works deal with subjects ranging from naval weapons to personal security. He is the author of *Small Arms Visual Encyclopedia*, *Tank[s] World War II*, and *Essential Weapons Identification Guide: Small Arms: 1945–Present*.